JUICY

OVER 200 JUICES & SMOOTHIES

igloo

JUICY

OVER 200 JUICES & SMOOTHIES

This edition published in 2009
by Igloo Books Ltd
Cottage Farm
Sywell
NN6 0BJ
www.igloo-books.com

10 9 8 7 6 5 4 3 2 1

ISBN: 978 1 84817 025 4

Project Managed by Toucan Books

Project Managed by Toucan Books

Author: Jacqueline Bellefontaine
Design and layout: Bradbury and Williams
Editor: Theresa Bebbington
Photography: Andrew Sydenham © Toucan Books
Proofreader: Marion Dent

Printed and manufactured in China

Contents

1
Life-Enhancing Drinks

"Juices" and "smoothies" are the new buzz words in the kitchen and for good reason too. For some time we have been told how important it is to eat a minimum of five fruit and vegetables every day. This is because they are packed full of the vitamins and minerals as well as the fibre that are required as part of a healthy diet. Juices and smoothies are a fun and tasty way of helping us to achieve this goal.

Homemade freshness

By making juices and smoothies yourself you will be ensuring that you get the maximum nutritional benefits from the fruit and vegetables. Shop-brought juices – even freshly squeezed juices – will have been in the bottle for several days, and in that time, the vitamin content will decrease. By making your own juices, you will know exactly what is in your drink, making it easier to avoid any additives. You may also prefer to use organic produce, thus ensuring that you are not inadvertently drinking any possible pesticide residues.

Curative powers

Juices have been used by herbalists and naturopaths for centuries to alleviate ailments and help prevent illness, and today many dieticians and nutritionists recommend including them in our diet. Juices and smoothies are a good way of consuming valuable antioxidants found in fruit and vegetables. Antioxidants help to protect our bodies against diseases and are important for the immune system.

Juices are also believed to be beneficial in many areas of health, from reducing stress and improving digestive health to helping build muscle and bone strength. The greater variety of fruit and vegetables in the diet, the more chance you have of consuming all the health-giving elements you'll need. If you tend to be a "meat and two veg person", making juices and smoothies is an easy way of extending the repertoire of fruit and vegetables you consume.

Whether you make juices and smoothies for health reasons or for fun, one thing is for certain – they are delicious and a great way of including fruit and vegetables in your diet.

Nutrition in a Nutshell

Smoothies vs. juices

The difference between a smoothie and a juice is that a smoothie contains the whole fruit and a juice contains just the juice of the fruit or vegetable. As a result a smoothie will contain more fibre and is the nutritional equivalent of eating the whole fruit. Fibre is important for good digestion and cardiovascular health. Smoothies are most often made from soft fruits such as strawberries, raspberries, blackberries, and grapes, which will easily blend to a puree. Juices can be made from hard fruits, including apples and pears, and vegetables. Juices do not contain the same fibre content as a smoothie, but a glass of juice can still be counted towards the recommended portions of fruit and vegetables per day.

Nutritional benefits

Juices and smoothies can help alleviate ailments, as well as help prevent illnesses, but don't wait until you feel below par to start enjoying the benefits of fresh fruit and vegetables. They are an important role in maintaining your general health.

Skin: Fruit and vegetables that are high in vitamin C help to build collagen, which is essential for general skin health. These include citrus fruit, strawberries, blackcurrants, peppers, and cabbage. Fruit and vegetables high in beta carotene such as apricots, carrots, squash, and spinach help protect the skin against sun damage. Vitamin E, which is found in nuts, seeds, dark green leafy vegetables, and wheat germ, helps protect against aging.

Hair and nails: Watercress, cucumber, and courgettes (zucchini) are good for healthy hair and nails.

Muscles and bones: Calcium is important for the healthy formation of bones and in the prevention of osteoporosis. It is found in milk and other dairy products, soy products, and broccoli. Vitamin K, found in leafy green vegetables, is also needed to maintain healthy bones.

Heart: Vitamin E, found in nuts, seeds, dark green leafy vegetables, and wheat germ, may help protect against heart disease. Garlic is also believed to be good for the heart. Fruit and vegetables high in beta carotene are required for a healthy heart too. Try apricots, dark leafy green vegetables, carrots, squash, and tomatoes.

Eyes: Choose fruit and vegetables high in beta carotene such as apricots, carrots, squash, blueberries, and spinach for good eye health. Vitamin C, found in many fruits and vegetables, is also known to help prevent the damage that leads to cataracts.

Stress: Grapes are good for their calming and restful qualities, as are oatmeal, celery, and chamomile. Foods that contain magnesium such as leafy green vegetables, nuts, and seeds will help reduce stress, as will those with the B vitamins (see page 11) and vitamin C. Try citrus fruit, berries, and peppers.

Energy: Pears, apples, bananas, and sweet potatoes are good for increasing energy levels. Orange and pineapple contain vitamin B_1, which is needed for energy production.

Detox: Fruit high in pectin or ellagic acid, including apples, strawberries, and grapes, are good for detoxing the body. Lemon and cranberry are good for the liver. Asparagus and garlic are good for cleaning the blood. Celery, cucumber, melon, and peaches have a diuretic effect and help prevent water retention. Cranberries and blueberries are good for the urinary tract.

Nausea and stomach problems: Ginger is a traditional remedy for nausea. Pineapple is good for the digestive tract, and fennel is great for digestion.

Immune system, colds, and flu: Include fruit and vegetables high in vitamin C and other antioxidants such as citrus fruit, berries – particularly dark red and purple berries such as blueberries and blackcurrants – peppers, spinach, and cherries. Broccoli and cabbage are believed to have cancer-preventing properties. Garlic and onions are good for colds, coughs, and flu.

Headaches: Fennel may help alleviate headaches. Cherries may have pain-relieving properties.

Vitamin and Mineral Sources

Although also present in other food sources, the following vitamins and minerals can be found in these fruit, vegetables, herbs and spices, dairy products, and nut and seed products used for making smoothies and juices.

Vitamins

A: Dairy products and dark green, orange, and yellow vegetables.
B$_1$: Cereals and nuts
B$_2$: Dairy products, broccoli, and spinach
Niacin: Cereals
B$_6$: Oats and peanuts
Folic acid (folate): Leafy green vegetables
B$_{12}$: Dairy products
C: Fruit and vegetables
E: Nuts, vegetables, and cereals
K: Leafy dark green vegetables

Minerals

Calcium: Dairy products and some vegetables
Magnesium: Nuts and seeds and green vegetables
Potassium: Nuts, onions, avocado, bananas and other fruit, and vegetables
Iron: Dark green vegetables and herbs
Zinc: Dairy products and cereals

Making Simple Juices

Some recipes for smoothies require the addition of fruit juices. You can use shop-bought juices, but if you have a juicer, you may want to make your own fresh juice for your smoothies, or you may simply want to make single fruit juices to drink. Here is a guide to how much juice you will get from the most popular fruit and vegetables.

To make 225ml/8floz/1 cup you will need:

Apple Juice: 4–5 apples
Orange Juice: 3–4 oranges
Pineapple Juice: ½ medium --pineapple
Tomato Juice: 4–6 medium tomatoes
Carrot Juice: 5–6 large carrots
Grapefruit Juice: 2 grapefruit
Grape Juice: 225–300g/8–10oz/
    2–2½ cups grapes
Mango Juice: 1½–2 mangoes
Pear Juice: 4–5 pears
Cherry Juice: 450–500g/1lb–1lb2oz/
    2–2½ cups cherries
Pomegranate Juice: 4–5 pomegranates

Use these quantities only as a guide. These juices were made using a centrifugal juicer (see pages 16–17). If you use a masticating juicer, you will get a larger quantity of juice because these machines are more efficient. Also remember that the amount of juice will vary between the different varieties of the same fruit and even from season to season. Ripe local fruits in season are usually juicier than fruits that have been picked unripe and flown across the world.

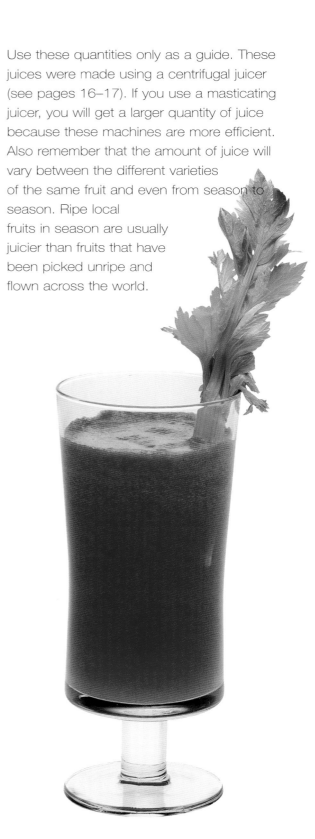

Juices Hints and Tips

Recipes make one to two glasses, depending on the size of your glass and the amount you want to drink. In general, vegetable juices are drunk in smaller quantities than fruit juices.

Stick to one type of measuring system. Never switch between them. Cup measurements are for standard American cups.

Always use fruit and vegetables that are in peak condition.

Wash fruit and vegetables well before use.

Prepare fruit and vegetables just before you need them. Some vitamins will start to be destroyed when you cut into the produce, and some fruit and vegetables discolor quickly.

Use organic ingredients if you want to avoid pesticide residues.

Cut vegetables into pieces that can be fed through the juicer's feeding tube easily. This will vary from machine to machine. Some machines will take whole apples, others will need the fruit or vegetables to be cut up in small pieces.

Insert soft fruit such as strawberries and blueberries slowly to extract the most juice. Follow soft fruit and leaves with a harder fruit such as an apple or a vegetable.

If you do need to store the juice, keep it in the refrigerator and add a few drops of lemon juice. (This will keep it from discoloring.)

Serve well chilled – use chilled vegetables and fruit or serve over ice.

Dilute juices for children with an equal quantity of water. You can use sparkling mineral water to create a fizzy fruit drink.

Fruit is high in fructose, a natural sugar, so people with diabetes should not drink too much. Dilute with water if necessary.

Do not drink more than 3 glasses of juice a day unless you are used to it – too much juice can cause an upset stomach.

Very dark vegetables such as beetroot (beet) and broccoli can have strong flavors. Dilute with water or with a milder flavored juice such as apple or celery if you want.

Smoothie Bases

Many smoothies are 100 percent fruit, but to blend efficiently a liquid is often added.

Fruit juice: In 100 percent fruit smoothies, fruit juice is added if necessary. If you have a juicer, juice your own fruit to maximize the vitamin content (see pages 12–13). For speed or convenience, you can use shop-brought juices. Chilled juices not made from concentrate have the best flavor.

Yogurt: When yogurt is added as a base it adds valuable calcium to the smoothie. Using a yogurt with live bacteria is good for the digestion, providing healthy bacteria. Greek-style yogurt will give the creamiest results but has the highest calorie content. Whole-milk yogurt can be used as a substitute for Greek-style yogurt. It adds more creaminess to the drink than a low-fat yogurt, with a calorie content that is higher than low-fat yogurt but not as high as Greek-style yogurt. Fruit-flavored yogurt may have a lot of added sugar.

Milk: Like yogurt, milk added to smoothies provides a good source of calcium. Calcium is important for growing children, and smoothies are a good way of including milk in a fussy child's diet. Whole-fat milk has the most flavor, but for those wishing to reduce fat content, skimmed or semi-skimmed milk is better.

Cream: For special occasions, adding single (light) or double (heavy) cream to a smoothie will give it a richer flavor.

Crème fraîche, fromage frais, quark, cottage cheese, mascarpone: These dairy products can be added to smoothies to provide calcium and as thickeners. The fat content varies and those with a high-fat content such as full-fat crème fraîche and mascarpone should be used in moderation. Low-fat crème fraîche, cottage cheese, and fromage frais can be used more frequently. Cottage cheese and other low-fat cheeses also add protein and make a smoothie more filling. They are good additions when a smoothie is being served in place of a full meal.

Ice Cream and sorbet: These can be added to smoothies for extra creaminess or flavor, as well as to to cool the drink. They can be blended with the fruit or added by the scoop in place of ice.

Dairy substitutes: Tofu is high in protein and low in fat. It is a good source of calcium and contains vitamin E. It has little flavor but will give your drink a more satisfying thickness and creamy texture.

Soy milk and soy yogurt can also be used as an alternative to dairy products, as can rice milk and oat milk. You can also use coconut milk, banana, and avocado to give smoothies a creamy texture and good flavor.

Smoothie Hints and Tips

Recipes make one to two glasses, depending on the size of your glass and the amount you want to drink.

Stick to one type of measuring system. Never switch between them. Cup measurements are for standard American cups.

Wash fruit and vegetables well. Peel if required and cut into chunks.

Use fruit and vegetables in peak condition.

Prepare fruit and vegetables just before you need them. Some vitamins start to be destroyed as you cut into the produce, and some produce discolors quickly.

Add liquids such as fruit juice, milk, or yogurt to the blender first.

For maximum nutritional benefit, serve the drinks immediately after preparing them.

Smoothies may separate on standing. This does not affect the flavor. Serve with a straw twizzler or spoon to stir before drinking.

Fresh ripe fruit should provide enough natural sweetness, but you can add a little extra sugar or honey to sweeten if required.

Keep berries and chopped up soft fruit such as apricots, peaches, and bananas in the freezer to make instant iced smoothies. They can go into the blender when frozen.

Smoothies are best served cold. Chill the ingredients before use and serve with plenty of ice. Crushed ice will cool a drink quickly. You can also use ice cream or sorbet.

Smoothies tend to be thick, but you can alter the thickness of the drink to your taste. Simply add extra milk, water, or fruit juice to achieve your preferred thickness.

If the smoothie is too thin, add a banana, which is a great thickener, or some frozen ingredients such as frozen fruit or ice cream. Or use cooked rice to thicken the smoothie.

You can remove seeds, pips, or fibrous material from the smoothie by straining through a nylon sieve. This will remove the fibre content, thus affecting the nutritional value of the drink, but it is useful if you find them unpleasant or you have fussy children.

Some liquids increase in volume and froth on blending so never overfill the blender.

Make sure the lid is firmly on your blender before processing.

Wash the blender as soon as possible after use. If fruit becomes dried on, soak in warm soapy water for a few minutes to soften the fruit.

Equipment

Whether you want to make juices, smoothies, or both, there is certain equipment that will be essential to have in your kitchen.

Juices

If you want to make juice from hard fruit and vegetables such as carrots, apples, and pears, you will need to invest in a juicer. There are two main types of juicers available.

Centrifugal juicer: This is the least expensive type and it works by finely grating the fruit or vegetables and then spinning them at high speed to separate the juice from the pulp, which is then discarded.

Masticating juicer: This machine is more efficient, but it comes with a higher price tag. It finely chops the fruit, then forces the juice out through a fine mesh.

Food processor: Some types have a centrifugal juicer attachment. It will not be as efficient as a dedicated machine; however, it will be more than adequate for occasional juicing.

Citrus juicer: Citrus juicer attachments are available for some juicers and food processors. These are specifically designed to squeeze juice from citrus fruit and are the most efficient equipment for juicing this kind of fruit. However, you can squeeze citrus fruit by simply peeling and feeding the segments through the juicers. Alternatively, you may prefer to use a simple hand lemon squeezer or reamer.

Smoothies

You may already have the equipment you need to make smoothies in your kitchen.

Blender: The best equipment for

making a smoothie is a blender, which consists of a jug placed on top of a motorized base, which powers the blades inside the jug. Use blenders for soft fruits such as strawberries and raspberries and always add some liquid to the jug.

Smoothie maker: This

specialized machine is a blender with a tap and nozzle at the base for easy pouring. It is not essential, but it will be a lot of fun and may encourage children to drink smoothies because they love to operate the tap.

Food processor: You can

use a food processor to make smoothies, although they generally tend to be less smooth. For the best results, add the fruit first and process before adding the liquid.

Electric wand:

This hand-held device will not be as efficient as a blender or food processor, but it is useful if you only make the occasional smoothie. You will need a deep bowl or jug for mixing.

Other Equipment

You will probably find most of the other equipment you require in your kitchen. Measuring jugs, cups, and spoons are useful to help ensure success every time.

You will need a chopping board and a sharp knife to prepare fruit and vegetables prior to juicing or making smoothies. For good hygiene practice, always use a separate board from one on which you prepare meat or fish.

A cherry stoner is useful if you want to make cherry juice.

A nylon sieve is useful to remove pips or seeds from smoothies or to make the smoothie thinner, but using one will remove some of the fibre from the juice.

2

Rise and Shine

Ruby Tuesday Pear Juice

2 pears, quartered
1 pomegranate
1 apple, quartered

1 Feed the pears through a juicer.

2 Cut the pomegranate in half and scoop out the flesh and seeds. Reserve a few seeds and feed the flesh and remaining seeds through the juicer.

3 Feed the apples through the juicer.

4 Pour into a glass and top with the reserved pomegranate seeds.

Long Ruby Tuesday Juice: Top up the juice with tonic, soda, or sparkling mineral water.

Spirulina, cholerella, and Klamath blue green algae,
available from health food shops, contain micronutrients and are sometimes referred to as super foods. They are a prefect addition to morning juices to give a real boost to your body's brain and nervous system.

Peach Divine

3 peaches, stoned
1 apple, quartered
1 banana, peeled
½ tsp spirulina, cholorella, or Klamath blue green algae (optional)

1 Place all the ingredients in a blender and blend until smooth.

2 Pour into a glass half-filled with ice.

Peach Divine II: Add 125ml/4floz/½ cup orange juice for a thinner smoothie.

Nectarine Divine: Replace the peaches with nectarines.

Super Veg Juice

1 red pepper, seeded and cut into strips
1 yellow pepper, seeded and cut into
   strips
Few spinach leaves
2 carrots, trimmed
3 sticks celery
¼ cucumber, peeled

1 Feed the vegetables in the order listed through a juicer.

2 Pour over ice in a glass.

Super Sweet Veg Juice: Add
1 peeled, cored, and seeded apple
to feed through the juicer.

Carrots are packed with
vitamin A, which will help
your skin stay healthy.

Frozen Berry Smoothie

115g/4oz/1 cup frozen mixed
   berries, such as raspberries,
   blueberries, and blackberries
225ml/8floz/1 cup milk
4 tbsp whole-milk yogurt
1 tbsp icing (confectioners') sugar

1 Place all the ingredients in a blender and blend until smooth.

2 If the smoothies are too thick, stir in a little extra milk.

3 Pour into tall glasses to serve.

Black Forest Berries: Add stoned
cherries to the frozen berry mixture (or
choose a mixture with cherries).

Dairy-Free Berry Smoothie: Replace
the milk with soy milk and yogurt with
50g/2oz/¼ cup silken tofu.

Berries are packed with **antioxidants**. Keep them in the freezer so you can enjoy their benefits any time of the year.

Spice 'n' Tropical

1 wedge pineapple, peeled and cut into
   chunks
½ small ripe mango, peeled, stoned,
   and cut into chunks
¼ papaya, peeled, seeded, and cut into
   chunks
1 small banana, peeled
Juice of ½ lime
Seeds of 3 cardamom pods, lightly
   crushed
Pinch ground chilli

1 Feed the prepared fruit through a juicer.

2 Stir in the cardamom and chilli, pour
into glasses, and serve.

Amazake is made from fermented grains, which convert starches to simpler natural sugars. It can create a sweet creamy texture without added sugar or dairy products.

Amazing Amazake Smoothie

6 to 8 apricots, stoned
125g/4oz/½ cup brown rice amazake
4 tbsp orange juice

1 Place all the ingredients in a blender
and blend until smooth.

2 Serve poured over ice.

Amazing Peach Amazake Smoothie:
Use 1 ripe peach instead of the apricots.

**Amazing Raspberry Amazake
Smoothie:** Use 50g/2oz/½ cup
raspberries in place of the apricots.

Muesli and Apple Smoothie

 This smoothie is ideal if you run out of fresh fruit because it uses **nutritious dried fruit.** However, if you do have some fresh berries, add a few to the smoothie to make it even more healthy.

5 no-soak dried apricots, chopped
5 no-soak dried pitted prunes, chopped
4 tbsp no-added sugar and salt muesli
1 tbsp maple syrup
225ml/8floz/1 cup apple juice

1 Place all the ingredients in a blender.

2 Blend until smooth. Add a little extra apple juice if the smoothie is too thick for your liking.

Warm Muesli and Apple Smoothie:
Gently heat the apple juice until just simmering before adding to the blender.

Muesli and Milk Smoothie: Use milk in place of the apple juice.

Carrot and Apple Juice

2 large carrots, trimmed
2 apples, cut into wedges

1 Feed the carrots and apples through a juicer.

2 Pour into glasses and serve.

Carrot, Apple, and Celery Juice: Add 2 sticks of celery to the juicer.

night vision booster

Spicy Tomato Juice

8 large ripe tomatoes, quartered
2 carrots, trimmed
4 spring onions (scallions), trimmed
2.5cm/1 inch piece of ginger root, peeled
½ chilli, seeded
1 red pepper, seeded and cut into strips
4 sticks celery
Celery sticks to serve

1 Feed the vegetables in the order listed through a juicer.

2 Pour into glass and serve with celery sticks to stir.

Seedy Tomato Juice: Sprinkle a few mixed seeds such as sesame, pumkin, and sunflower seeds over the drink for extra nutritional benefits.

Easy Tropical

¼ small pineapple, peeled and cut into
   chunks
1 banana, peeled
125ml/4floz/½ cup apple and mango
   juice

1 Reserve a piece of pineapple and a
   slice of banana to decorate if desired.
   Place all the ingredients in a blender and
   blend until smooth.

2 Pour into a glass and decorate with
   the reserved fruit to serve.

Really Tropical: Add ¼ papaya,
seeded and cut into chunks, to
the blender.

Banana and Blueberry Yognog

1 banana, peeled
50g/2oz/½ cup blueberries
225ml/8floz/1 cup natural (plain) yogurt

1 Place all the ingredients in a blender and blend until smooth.

2 Pour into a glass and serve.

Banana and Raspberry Yognog: Use raspberries in place of blueberries.

Oatmeal releases energy slowly. Bananas have simple and complex carbohydrates and give instant energy without the blood sugar crash. This smoothie will keep you going until lunch time.

Banana and Oatmeal Smoothie

1 tbsp fine oatmeal
1 ripe banana
1 tsp clear honey
½ tsp vanilla essence (extract), optional
4 tbsp natural (plain) yogurt

1 Place the oatmeal in a blender and pour in 125ml/4floz/½ cup boiling water. Allow to stand for 10 minutes.

2 Reserve a slice of banana. Place the remainder in the blender with the rest of the ingredients and 125ml/4floz/½ cup cold water. Blend until smooth.

3 Pour into a glass and decorate with the banana slice.

Strawberry and Oatmeal Smoothie: Add 115g/4oz/1 cup strawberries instead of the banana.

Mango Lassi

1 ripe mango, peeled, stoned, and cut
  into chunks
350ml/12floz/1½ cups whole-milk
  natural (plain) yogurt
Crushed ice

1 Place the mango and yogurt in a
  blender and whiz until smooth.

2 Pour over crushed ice in a glass
  to serve.

Banana Lassi: Replace the mango with
1 large, ripe peeled banana.

Spicy Lassi: Add ½ tsp ground
cinnamon and ¼ tsp grated nutmeg
to either the mango or banana lassi.

Banana and Coffee Morning Wake Up

1 ripe banana, peeled
125ml/4floz/½ cup strong hot coffee
125ml/4floz/½ cup hot milk

1 Place the banana in a blender with the coffee and blend until well combined.

2 Carefully add the hot milk and blend briefly to combine.

3 Pour into heat-proof glasses and serve.

Iced Banana and Coffee Wake Up:
Make the coffee and chill well. Proceed as above, adding a handful of ice to the blender with the banana and using chilled milk.

A meal in a glass is an ideal **substitute for breakfast.** The muesli provides quick and slow-release energy, the berries add valuable vitamins, and the yogurt and milk supply calcium.

Breakfast In a Glass

4 tbsp no-added sugar and salt muesli
1 tbsp maple syrup
Few blueberries
Few raspberries
225ml/8oz/1 cup natural (plain) yogurt
125ml/4floz/½ cup skimmed milk

1 Place all the ingredients in a blender and blend until smooth.

2 Pour into a glass and serve.

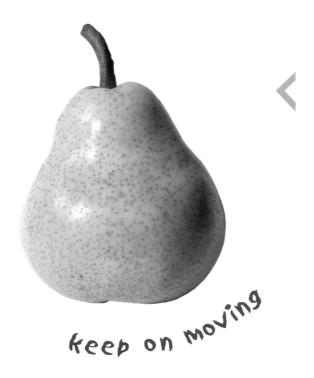

Pears are great energizers because instead of creating a sudden burst of energy, they release energy slowly.

keep on moving

Raspberry, Pear, and Almond Smoothie

2 pears, cut into wedges
1 orange, peeled and segmented
175g/6oz/1½ cups raspberries
4 tbsp ground almonds

1 Feed the pears and orange through a juicer and pour the juice into a blender.

2 Add the raspberries and ground almonds and blend until smooth.

Blackberry, Pear, and Almond Smoothie. Replace the raspberries with blackberries.

Strawberry, Pear, and Almond Smoothie: Replace the raspberries with strawberries.

Pear and Apricot Juice

2 pears, cut into wedges
1 apple, cut into wedges
6 apricots, stoned

1 Feed the fruit through a juicer.

2 Pour into a glass and serve immediately.

Apple and Apricot Juice: Instead of combining pears with an apple, use only apples – you'll need 3 apples.

Spinach and Pepper Punch

150g/5oz/3 cups baby spinach leaves
2 yellow peppers, seeded and cut into
strips

1 Reserve a couple of strips of pepper.
Feed the spinach and peppers through
a juicer.

2 Pour into glasses and serve with the
reserved sticks of pepper.

Creamy Spinach and Pepper Punch:
Stir the juice into 125ml/4floz/½ cup
natural (plain) yogurt.

This juice is power packed
with vital nutrients, making it a perfect
start to the day.

Strawberry and Vanilla Shake

115g/4oz/1 cup strawberries, washed
  and hulled
225ml/8floz/1 cup milk
4 tbsp vanilla-flavored yogurt
½ tsp vanilla essence (extract)

1 Reserve a strawberry to decorate. Place
all the ingredients in a blender and blend
until smooth. If the smoothie is too thick,
stir in a little extra milk.

2 Pour into a tall glass and decorate with
a strawberry to serve.

Raspberry and Vanilla Shake: Use
raspberries in place of the strawberries.

Blackberry and Vanilla Shake: Use
blackberries in place of the strawberries.

3

Liquid Lunch

Open Sesame Vegetable Juice

4 carrots, about 400g/14oz in weight
115g/4oz/¾ cup green beans (string beans), trimmed
1 tbsp tahini
Few toasted sesame seeds

1 Feed the carrots and beans through a juicer.

2 Stir in the tahini until well combined. If it is too thick, thin it with a little warm water before adding it to the juice.

3 Pour into glasses and sprinkle with sesame seeds.

Meal in One: If serving as a meal substitute, whisk in some soft tofu to provide protein.

Sesame seeds contain valuable nutrients, particularly calcium, which strengthens bones, as well as iron, vitamin E, and protein. Tahini is made from sesame seeds ground to a paste.

Winter Winner

1 large parsnip, trimmed
2 carrots, trimmed
Small handful coriander (cilantro)
1 small bulb fennel, cut into chunks
2 crisp green apples, quartered

1 Feed the parsnips and carrots through the juicer.

2 Feed the coriander (cilantro) through the juicer, followed by the fennel and apple.

3 Pour into glasses and serve.

Winter Winner Basilico: Use basil in place of the coriander.

Celery Winner: Replace the fennel with 4 or 5 sticks of celery.

keep yourself strong

Smokin' Red Pepper Juice

2 red peppers, seeded and cut
into strips
1 large courgette (zucchini)
1 clove garlic
1 orange, peeled and segmented
½ tsp smoked paprika

1 Feed the pepper, courgette (zucchini), garlic, and orange segments through a juicer.

2 Stir in the smoked paprika and serve.

Sunny Smokin' Pepper Juice: Use yellow or orange peppers in place of the red pepper.

Rosy Smokin' Pepper Juice: Add 1 medium ripe tomato.

Totally Tropical Juice

½ mango, peeled and cut into chunks
¼ papaya, seeded, peeled, and cut
   into chunks
1 wedge pineapple, peeled and cut
   into chunks
1 kiwi fruit, peeled and cut
   into wedges
1 banana, peeled
1 passion fruit
1–2 slices star fruit (optional)

1 Feed the first five fruits through
a juicer in the order listed.

2 Pour into a glass.

3 Cut the passion fruit in half,
scoop out the seeds, and stir
   into the juice.

4 Decorate the glass with the star
fruit if desired.

Totally Tropical Smoothie: All the fruit
can be placed in a blender for
a super thick smoothie.

Carrot, Beetroot, and Ginger Juice

2 large carrots, trimmed
1cm/½ inch piece of ginger root, peeled
1 beetroot (beet), washed and trimmed

1 Feed the carrots, ginger, and then the beetroot (beet) through a juicer.

2 Serve well chilled.

Carrot, Beetroot, and Celery Juice:
Replace the ginger with 2 sticks of celery.

tame your tummy

Chilli Mango and Lime Smoothie

1 ripe mango, peeled, stoned and cut into chunks
2 limes
1 small red chilli, seeded and chopped
Few fresh mint leaves

1 Place the mango in a blender.

2 Squeeze the juice from the limes and add to the blender. Then add the chilli.

3 Blend until smooth.

4 Pour into a glass and top with a few small mint leaves.

Minty Mango and Lime Smoothie:
Replace the chilli with a few fresh mint leaves.

Waldorf Juice

4 sticks celery, cut into short lengths
2 tbsp raisins
1 tbsp walnuts
1 crisp apple, cut into wedges
1 tbsp low-fat fromage frais (yogurt) or
   crème fraîche (optional)
Celery sticks to stir

1 Feed the celery, raisins, walnuts, and
apple through the juicer.

2 Serve topped with the fromage frais
(yogurt) or crème fraîche and a
celery stick to stir.

Sweet Waldorf Juice: Add a carrot for
a slightly sweeter juice.

Cardamom is an aid to
digestion, and it is also thought
to help battle colds, fevers,
inflammatory conditions, and liver
problems. Ricotta cheese is a
good source of calcium.

Creamy Orange Delight

3 cardamom pods
115g/4oz/⅛ cup ricotta cheese
225ml/8floz/1 cup freshly squeezed
orange juice
1–2 tsp clear honey

1 Remove the seeds from the cardamom
pods and grind in a pestle and mortar.

2 Place in a blender with the ricotta
cheese and blend.

3 With the motor running, gradually pour in
the orange juice.

4 Sweeten with honey and serve over ice
if desired.

Pumpkin Pie Smoothie

150g/5oz/1¼ cups pumpkin flesh,
   cubed
¼ tsp ground cinnamon
Pinch grated nutmeg
1 small red chilli, seeded and chopped
225ml/8floz/1 cup orange juice

1   Steam the pumpkin for 10 minutes until just tender and let cool.

2   Place in a blender with the remaining ingredients. Blend until smooth.

3   Chill well and serve cold.

Spicy Squash Smoothie: Use a butternut squash instead of the pumpkin.

Cool Avocado Angel

1 avocado, peeled and stoned
½ cucumber, peeled and cut into
   chunks
225ml/8floz/1cup orange juice

1   Place all the ingredients in a blender and blend until smooth.

2   Pour into glasses half-filled with ice and serve.

Avocado Devil: Add 1 seeded, chopped red chilli to the mix to spice up the smoothie.

A super-charged avocado adds thickness to this smoothie. Avocado is an excellent source of potassium, folic acid (folate), and vitamin A, as well as protein, iron, and other vitamins and minerals.

sing from the heart

Deep Purple Smoothie

115g/4oz/¾ cup black or green grapes
115g/4oz/1 cup cherries, pitted
125ml/4floz/½ cup cranberry juice
Few cherries to serve

1 Feed the grapes through a juicer.

2 Add the grape juice, cherries, and
   cranberry juice to a blender and blend
   until smooth.

3 Pour over ice in glasses, decorate with a
   few cherries, and serve.

Nutty Banana Smoothie

1 banana
225ml/8floz/1 cup milk
1 tbsp smooth peanut butter

1 Peel and slice the banana, wrap it in
   clingfilm (plastic wrap), and freeze
   overnight.

2 Place all the ingredients in a blender
   and blend until smooth.

3 Pour in a glass and serve immediately.

Banana and Sesame Smoothie:
Instead of peanut butter use 2 tsp tahini.

Health in a Glass

2 medium tomatoes
210g/7½oz/3 cups cabbage,
   thickly shredded
Handful of parsley
Celery stick to serve

1 Feed the tomatoes, cabbage, and parsley through a juicer.

2 Pour into a glass and add a celery stick before serving.

Liquorice Liquor: Replace the parsley with 1 small bulb of fennel, cut into chunks.

Spinach is a good source of folic acid (folate), which is especially important for pregnant women. The tomatoes provide vitamin C, which helps to unlock the iron and calcium in spinach.

Green Giant Juice

2 medium tomatoes
150g/5oz/1¾ cups broccoli
150g/5oz/3 cups spinach

1 Cut a few slices from the tomato and reserve. Feed the tomatoes, broccoli, and spinach through a juicer.

2 Pour over ice in glasses and decorate with the tomato slices before serving.

Spiced Green Giant Juice: Add a pinch of grated nutmeg for some spice.

Strawberry and Mint Smoothie

115g/4oz/1 cup strawberries, washed
  and hulled
225ml/8floz/1 cup soy milk
85g/3oz/⅓ cup firm tofu
10 mint leaves, chopped
Mint leaves to decorate

1 Place all the strawberries, soy milk, and tofu in a blender. Add the chopped mint and blend until smooth. If the smoothies are too thick, stir in a little extra soy milk.

2 Pour into tall glasses and decorate with whole mint leaves to serve.

Raspberry and Mint Smoothie: Use raspberries instead of strawberries.

Blackberry and Mint Smoothie: Use blackberries instead of strawberries.

liquid lunch

Creamy Borscht

3 small beetroots (beets)
4 spring onions (scallions), trimmed
2 tsp lemon juice
85ml/3floz/¾ cup fromage frais (yogurt)
  or double (heavy) cream
Few chives, snipped

1 Feed the beetroots (beets) and onions (scallions) through a juicer.

2 Stir in the lemon juice and fromage frais (yogurt) or cream.

3 Pour into glasses and sprinkle with the snipped chives.

Borscht with a Kick: Add 1 tbsp dry sherry to the juice.

Slim 'n' Creamy Borscht: Use low-fat fromage frais or low-fat natural (plain) yogurt instead of the regular fromage frais or cream.

Beetroots (beets) are a good source of folic acid (folate) and vitamin C, and some people believe they have curative powers to relieve headaches and other aches and pains.

Banana Date Smoothie

125ml/4floz/½ cup milk
4 tbsp yogurt
1 tbsp date syrup
1 banana, peeled
4 dates, stoned and chopped
2 tsp wheat germ

1 Place all the ingredients in a blender and blend until smooth.

2 Pour into a glass and serve.

Dairy-free Banana Date Smoothie:
Use soy milk to replace the milk and yogurt for a dairy-free smoothie.

Wheat germ contains valuable B vitamins. Date syrup is a great way to add sweetness without adding sugar.

Gazpacho Smoothie

¼ red pepper
¼ green pepper
¼ red onion, peeled
¼ cucumber
1 clove garlic
Few sprigs parsley
1 tsp red wine vinegar
225ml/8floz/1 cup tomato juice
5 tbsp cold water
Dash Tabasco sauce
Freshly ground black pepper
Cucumber and parsley to decorate

1 Place all the ingredients in a blender and blend until smooth.

2 Serve chilled, decorated with slices of cucumber and a few parsley leaves.

The most colorful peppers provide the most bioflavonoids, which may help prevent cancer. Red peppers have more antioxidants than green peppers, but green peppers have more vitamin C than red peppers.

Lemongrass and Lime Smoothie

1 stick lemongrass
1 lime
2 tsp wheat germ
225ml/8floz/1cup whole-milk yogurt
1–2 tsp clear honey

1 Trim the ends of the lemon grass and remove the tough outer layers. Thinly slice the remainder; place in a blender.

2 Grate the zest from the lime and squeeze the juice. Add the zest and juice to the blender and blend until the lemon grass is finely chopped.

3 Add the wheat germ, yogurt, and honey and blend until smooth.

Lemongrass and Orange Smoothie: For a sweeter smoothie, replace the lime with 1 orange or 2 tangerines.

Peach and Almond Smoothie

2 peaches, stoned
2 tbsp toasted flaked almonds
225ml/8floz/1 cup freshly squeezed orange juice

1 Place the peaches and almonds in a blender and blend until smooth.

2 Add the orange juice and blend again.

3 Pour into glasses to serve.

Peach and Cashew Smoothie: Use lightly toasted cashew nuts instead of the almonds.

Peach and Hazelnut Smoothie: Use lightly toasted hazelnuts instead of the almonds.

Wheat germ is packed full of calcium, and it has the B vitamins, vitamin E, magnesium, iron, and zinc, making this a nutritious ingredient.

Red Slaw Juice

½ small red cabbage, thickly shredded

1 carrot, trimmed

1 tbsp seedless raisins

2 apples, quartered

1 tbsp lemon juice

1 Feed the cabbage, carrot, raisins, and apples through a juicer.

2 Stir in the lemon juice and serve.

Nutty Slaw Juice: Grind a few shelled walnuts and add to the juice.

Fig and Apricot Smoothie

3 large figs, trimmed and quartered

4 apricots, stoned

1 tbsp wheat germ or oatmeal

125ml/4floz/½ cup freshly squeezed orange juice

1 tbsp lemon juice, freshly squeezed

1 Place all the ingredients in a blender and blend until smooth.

2 Pour into glasses and serve.

Fig and Date Smoothie: Replace the apricots with fresh pitted dates.

keep your tummy happy

Lime and Passion Fruit Cooler

1 lime
4 passion fruit
125ml/4floz/½ cup apple juice

1 Grate the zest from one lime and place in a blender. Cut the pith and peel away from the lime, then add the flesh to the blender.

2 Scoop out the passion fruit seeds into the blender, add the apple juice, and blend briefly.

3 Strain through a nylon sieve, pour into a glass, and serve.

Orange and Passion Fruit Cooler: Replace lime zest with orange zest and replace the apple juice with orange juice.

Tofu Cooler: Add 115g/4oz/½ cup silken tofu with the apple juice.

Carrot, Apple, and Ginger Juice

2 large carrots, trimmed and cut
  into chunks
2 apples, quartered
1cm/½ inch piece of ginger root, peeled
Carrot sticks to serve

1 Feed the carrot, apple, and ginger through a juicer.

2 Pour into glasses, add carrot sticks to stir, and serve.

Carrot, Apple, and Chilli Juice:
Replace the ginger with a small seeded chilli for a real zip.

Ginger can help to relieve nausea and morning sickness.

4

Bedtime Soothers

Make a Date with Sleep Smoothie

1 banana, peeled
115g/4oz/½ cup amazake
4 fresh dates, stoned and chopped
125ml/4floz/½ cup milk or soy milk
Freshly grated nutmeg

1 Place the banana, amazake, and dates in a blender and blend until smooth.

2 Thin with milk or soy milk to your preferred consistency.

3 Sprinkle generously with nutmeg.

Dairy-Free Banana and Date Smoothie: Replace the milk with apple juice for a dairy-free alternative.

Banana and Raisin Smoothie: You can use 2 tbsp of seedless raisins instead of the dates.

Bananas contain the amino acid tryptophan, which helps you sleep, and nutmeg has phytochemicals, which also aid sleep.

Sleep Easy

1 tbsp fine oatmeal
80ml/2⅔floz/⅓ cup boiling water
90g/3½oz/1¾ cups iceberg lettuce
2 sticks celery
2 carrots

1 Place the oatmeal in a blender and pour the boiling water it. Let cool.

2 Feed the remaining ingredients through a juicer and stir into the oatmeal mixture.

Tomtato Sleep Easy: Replace the carrots with 1 large tomato.

Nutmeg has **calming** properties and the other spices help to give this drink a warming cosy spiciness. The oats will help to stave off any hunger pangs until morning.

Hot Choc Froth

350ml/12floz/1½ cups milk
1 tbsp cocoa powder
50g/2oz plain (dark) chocolate, broken
  into chunks
1 tbsp icing (confectioners') sugar
Few mini marshmallows

1 Place the milk in a small pan and heat until almost boiling.

2 Place the cocoa, chocolate, and sugar in a blender and carefully pour in half the hot milk. Blend until smooth.

3 Add the remaining milk and blend until frothy.

4 Pour into two heatproof glasses or mugs and top with marshmallows.

Almond Choc Froth: Add 25g/1oz Amaretti biscuits and ½ tsp almond essence (extract) if desired.

Hot & Spicy Apple Sleepy

2 apples, peeled, cored, and sliced
50g/2oz/¼ cup raisins
2 tbsp rolled oats
¼ tsp each ground cardamom,
  cinnamon, and nutmeg
Extra nutmeg to serve

1 Place the apples, raisins, oats, and 350ml/12floz/1½ cups of water into a small saucepan.

2 Bring to the boil, then reduce the heat and simmer gently for 5 minutes. Stir in the spices.

3 Let cool slightly, then carefully pour into a blender and blend at a low speed until smooth.

4 Pour into heatproof cups and sprinkle a little nutmeg over each drink before serving.

Chilled Spicy Apple Smoothie: Chill the apple smoothie and serve cold.

Banana Wind-Down Smoothie

Seeds of two cardamom pods
1 banana, peeled
225ml/8floz/1 cup freshly squeezed
    orange juice

1 Crush the cardamom seeds with a pestle and mortar; place in a blender.

2 Add the banana and orange juice, and blend until smooth.

3 Pour into a glass and serve.

Pineapple Wind-Down Smoothie:
Use a wedge of trimmed pineapple instead of the banana.

Chamomile is known for its **restful, soothing** qualities, and it also has anti-inflammatory and antispasmodic properties that can help to settle digestive problems.

Chamomile, Orange, and Elderflower Soother

1 chamomile teabag
1 orange
1 tbsp elderflower cordial

1 Place the teabag in a heatproof jug and cover with 225ml/8floz/1 cup of boiling water; let steep for 10 minutes.

2 Remove the teabag and discard.

3 Squeeze the juice from the orange and add to the tea. Add the elderflower cordial and stir.

4 Pour into a glass and serve immediately.

Chamomile, Orange, and Blackcurrant Soother: Use a blackcurrant cordial in place of the elderflower cordial.

get peeled and feel great

Grape Slumber Juice

225g/8oz/1 cup red or green grapes
2 oranges, peeled and segmented
1 tsp lemon juice

1 Feed the grapes through a juicer, followed by the orange segments.

2 Stir in the lemon juice and serve.

Brandied Grape and Orange Juice:
Add 2 tbsp brandy to the juice.

Oat-So-Sleepy Banana Smoothie

1 tbsp fine oatmeal
225ml/8floz/1 cup milk
50g/2oz/¼ cup seedless raisins
1 small ripe banana, peeled
1 tsp clear honey

1 Place the oatmeal in small pan with the milk and bring almost to the boil, stirring occasionally.

2 Carefully pour into a blender, add the remaining ingredients, and blend until the mixture is smooth.

3 Pour into a heatproof glass or mug and serve.

Dairy-Free Oat-So-Sleepy Smoothie:
Replace the milk with soy milk.

Milk contains **tryptophan**, an essential amino acid that is a natural sleep inducer. If a skin forms over the milk, don't throw it away. Add it to the blender – the skin contains valuable nutrients.

Yogurt is full of **calcium** for healthy bones. Seeds add valuable good fats.

Honey Yogurt Flip

225ml/8floz/1 cup low-fat natural (plain) yogurt
2 tbsp clear honey
1 tbsp toasted mixed seeds such as pumpkin, sesame, and sunflower seeds
Ground cinnamon

1 Place the yogurt, honey, and half the seeds in a blender and blend briefly.

2 Pour into a glass and top with the remaining seeds. Sprinkle with cinnamon and serve.

Apple Honey Yogurt Flip: Add 1 peeled and cored apple to the blender.

Banana Honey Yogurt Flip: Add 1 small peeled banana to the blender.

Celery is known to have a calming restful effect and this juice should help to **promote sleep**.

Carrot and Celery Calmer

6 sticks celery, trimmed
4 carrots, trimmed
Carrot and celery sticks to serve

1 Feed the celery and carrots through a juicer and pour into glasses.

2 Serve with carrot and celery sticks.

Apple and Celery Calmer: Use 2 apples in place of the carrots.

5
Drinks for Dieters

Apple Power Booster

body-soothing king

85g/3oz/¾ cup rocket (arugula) leaves
1 handful watercress
1 apple, quartered
1 stick celery, with its leaves

1 Feed the rocket (arugula) and watercress through a juicer, followed by the apple and celery.

2 Pour into glasses and serve.

Garlicky Apple Power: Omit the rocket and watercress, use 2 apples, and add 1 clove of peeled garlic.

Spinach Power Booster: Use spinach in place of the rocket.

Watercress is rich in antioxidants, which can help prevent cancer and some other diseases. Watercress is also a good source of vitamins A and C.

Passionate Mango Smoothie

2 passion fruits
1 mango, stoned and peeled
125ml/4floz/½ cup low-fat natural
  (plain) yogurt
225/8floz/1 cup skimmed milk
Few ice cubes

1 Scoop the flesh and seeds out of the passion fruits and feed through a juicer with the mango.

2 Place the passion fruit and mango juice in a blender, along with the remaining ingredients, and blend until smooth.

3 Pour into a glass and serve.

Blackberry Delight

1 banana, peeled
115g/4oz/1 cup blackberries
175ml/6floz/¾ cup apple juice

1 Reserve 1 or 2 blackberries and 1 or 2 slices of banana to decorate. Place all the ingredients in a blender and blend until smooth.

2 Pour into tall glasses and decorate with the reserved fruit.

Raspberry Delight: Replace the blackberries with raspberries.

Raspberry and Orange Delight: Replace the blackberries with raspberries and use orange juice instead of the apple juice.

Basil and Orange Juice

4 oranges, peeled and segmented
Small handful basil leaves
Orange slice and basil leaves to serve

1 Feed half the oranges through a juicer, then add the basil leaves, followed by the remaining orange segments.

2 Pour into a glass and decorate with the orange slice and basil leaves.

Tomato and Basil Juice: Instead of the oranges, use 4 large or 6 medium ripe tomatoes. Feed half the tomatoes through the juicer, then add the basil, followed by the remaining tomatoes.

Orange and Parsley Juice: Use parsley in place of the basil.

Tomato and Parsley Juice: Use tomatoes and parsley and proceed as for Tomato and Basil Juice.

The beneficial volatile oils found in basil have antibacterial properties and can provide anti-inflammatory benefits. Basil is also a good source of beta carotene.

Carrot and Spinach Zing

6 carrots, trimmed
115g/4oz/1 cup spinach leaves
2.5cm/1 inch piece of ginger root,
   peeled
1 tsp Klamath blue green algae
   (optional)

1 Feed the carrots, spinach, and ginger
through a juicer.

2 Stir in the Klamath blue green algae if
using and serve over ice.

Carrot and Rocket Zing: Use rocket
(arugula) in place of the spinach.

Carrot and Watercress Zing: Use
watercress in place of the spinach.

Slimmer's Lassi

1 mango, stoned
225ml/8floz/1 cup low-fat natural
   (plain) yogurt
125ml/4floz/½ cup skimmed milk
Crushed ice

1 Place the mango, yogurt, and milk in a
blender and blend until smooth.

2 Pour over crushed ice to serve.

Slimmer's Banana Lassi: Replace the
mango with 1 large, ripe peeled banana.

Slimmer's Berry Lassi: Instead of
the mango, use 115g/4oz/¾–1 cup
of fresh berries.

Klamath blue green
algae is packed with protein
and minerals that are good for the
body. It helps stop food cravings,
which makes it ideal when dieting.

Cucumber is a good **diuretic**, so it can help stop water retention and aid weight loss. Cucumber also helps to lower blood pressure.

Melon and Cucumber Cooler

½ small honeydew melon, peeled, seeded, and cut into chunks
½ cucumber
Sparkling mineral water (optional)

1 Place the melon and cucumber in a blender and blend until smooth.

2 Pour into glasses.

3 Dilute with sparkling mineral water if required.

Melon, Cucumber, and Celery Cooler: Add 2 sticks of celery.

Watermelon and Orange Smoothie

450g/1lb/3 cups watermelon, peeled and cut into chunks
4 oranges

1 Discard most of the seeds and place the watermelon in a blender.

2 Squeeze the juice from the oranges and add to the blender.

3 Blend until smooth and serve over ice.

Watermelon and Lemon Smoothie: Instead of 4 oranges use 2 oranges and 2 lemons for a tangier flavor.

Melon and Orange Smoothie: Use honeydew, canteloupe, or another variety of melon instead of watermelon.

vitamin-packed

This is a fabulous low-cal drink that can be enjoyed any time of the day.

>

Watermelon and Ginger Refresher

450g/1lb/3 cups watermelon, peeled
   and cut into chunks
1cm/½ inch piece of ginger root, peeled
A little lemon juice
Sugar to taste

1 Feed the watermelon, followed by the ginger, through a juicer. Or blend in a blender, but grate the ginger first.

2 Pour into glasses and stir in a little lemon juice. Sweeten with a little sugar if required.

Melon and Ginger Refresher: Use a different variety of melon such as galia or honeydew melon.

Celery and Rocket Lift

2 sticks celery
Handful of rocket (arugula) leaves
225g/8oz/1 cup green grapes
Celery sticks to serve

1 Feed the ingredients through a juicer in the order listed.

2 Pour over crushed ice and add the celery sticks to stir.

Snappy Celery and Rocket Lift:
Add a few sugar snap pea pods after the grapes.

Pineapple is a good source for vitamin C and **bromelain**, which can help heal to wounds.

Summer Surprise

½ melon, seeded, peeled, and cut into chunks
½ pineapple, peeled and cut into chunks
1 mango, stoned and cut into chunks
115g/4oz/1 cup blueberries
1 tsp Klamath blue green algae (optional)

1 Place all the ingredients in a blender and blend until smooth.

2 Pour into glasses filled with plenty of ice.

Berry Surprise: Replace the blueberries, with strawberries, raspberries, or other berries of your choice.

Apricot and Prune Stand-By

6 pitted prunes, chopped
400g/14oz can apricots, in their juice

1 Place the ingredients in a blender and blend until smooth.

2 Serve over ice.

Peach and Prune Stand-By: Replace the canned apricots with canned peaches.

Pear and Prune Stand-By: Use canned pears instead of the apricots.

Prunes are an **appetite suppressant**, so they are a perfect start to the day if you are watching the scales.

kung fu bad bacteria

Prune, Apple, and Pear Juice

12 prunes, pitted
2 apples, quartered
2 pears, quartered

1 Place the prunes in a heatproof bowl and cover with 125ml/4floz/½ cup boiling water. Let stand for 20 minutes.

2 Feed the apples through a juicer, followed by the soaked prunes and soaking water and then the pears.

3 Chill before serving.

Apricot, Apple, and Pear Juice: Replace the prunes with 8 stoned dried apricots.

Tomato Treat

8 medium tomatoes
Small handful fresh basil leaves
125ml/4floz/½ cup low-fat natural (plain) yogurt
115g/4oz/½ cup low-fat cottage cheese
1 tsp brewer's yeast, optional
2 sticks celery to serve

1 Place the tomatoes, basil, yogurt, cottage cheese, and brewer's yeast in a blender and blend until smooth.

2 Pour into glasses and serve with the celery sticks to stir.

Spicy Tomato Treat: Add ½ of a seeded red chilli for a little extra zing.

Salad Treat: Add ¼ of a cucumber, cut into chunks.

 This low-calorie smoothie has **brewer's yeast**, a valuable vegetarian source for the B vitamins, iron, and zinc – all vital for a well-balanced diet.

Blackberry and Apple Juice

225g/8oz/1¾ cups blackberries
2 apples, cut into wedges

1 Reserve a few blackberries
and slices of apple for
decoration. Feed
the blackberries
and apples through
a juicer.

2 Pour into glasses
and decorate with
the reserved fruit.

**Raspberry and Apple
Juice:** Replace the
blackberries with
raspberries.

Cranberries can help prevent or alleviate cystitis and other urinary tract infections. They can also help prevent kidney and bladder stones.

Peachy Cranberry Fizz

115g/4oz/1 cup cranberries
1 tbsp caster (superfine) sugar
2 peaches, stoned
225ml/8floz/1 cup freshly squeezed orange juice
Clear honey or maple syrup, if desired
Sparkling mineral water to serve

1 Place the cranberries in a small pan with the sugar and 2 tbsp water. Cook for about 5 minutes until soft, then let cool.

2 Cut the peaches into pieces and place in a blender with the cranberries and orange juice. Add a little honey or maple syrup if you want a sweeter drink. Blend until smooth.

3 Strain through a nylon sieve, if desired, to remove the seeds.

4 Pour into glasses and top up with the mineral water.

Nectarine and Cranberry Fizz: Use nectarines in place of the peaches.

Plum and Cranberry Fizz: Use 8–12 plums in place of the peaches.

6

Body
Boosters

Pineapple and Papaya Power

½ pineapple, peeled and cut into chunks
½ papaya, peeled and cut into chunks
1 apple, quartered

1 Feed the fruit through a juicer.

2 Pour into glasses and serve immediately.

Pineapple Power Smoothie: Blend the pineapple and papaya in a blender with 125ml/4floz/½ cup orange juice.

 Bromelain found in pineapple reduces bruising so if you have taken a knock or a fall, try this juice to get you back on your feet.

bruise buster

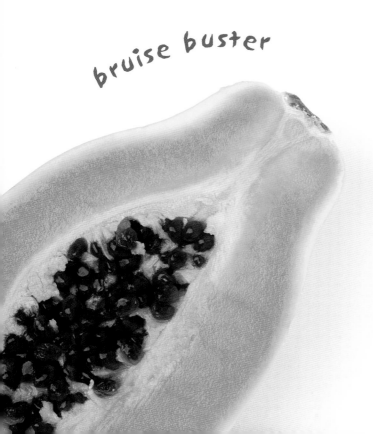

Nutty Bananas for the Muscles

1 medium banana, peeled
175ml/6floz/¾ cup soy milk
4 tbsp ground almonds
Few ice cubes
Cinnamon stick to serve

1 Place the banana, soy milk, ground almond, and ice cubes in a blender. Blend until smooth.

2 Pour into a glass and add a cinnamon stick to stir.

This is a great **detox** juice. The Klamath has protein and minerals that will give your body a boost.

Cool Customer

4 apples, quartered
2 carrots, trimmed
1 stick celery
½ cucumber, peeled
1 tsp Klamath blue green algae (optional)
Cucumber slices to serve

1 Feed all the vegetables through a juicer and stir in the Klamath algae.

2 Pour over ice, decorate with cucumber slices, and serve.

Fruit and Cool: Replace the carrots with 2 pears for a fruity detox juice.

Pineapple Ginger Calmer

¼ pineapple, peeled
2.5cm/1 inch piece of ginger root, peeled
1 tbsp clear honey
Seeds of 4 cardamom pods, crushed
Strips of ginger stem or pinch of grated
    nutmeg to serve

1 Place all the ingredients in a blender
with 125ml/4 floz/½ cup of water. Blend
until smooth.

2 Thin the smoothie down to a desired
consistency with more water. If you have
an upset stomach, dilute the smoothie
and drink slowly.

3 Pour into a glass and decorate with the
strips of stem ginger or sprinkle with
nutmeg if desired.

Papaya Ginger Calmer: Use 1 papaya
in place of the pineapple.

For an upset stomach,
this drink contains pineapple,
which can help the digestive tract,
ginger, and cardamom, which can
relieve vomiting.

Citrus fruit such as grapefruit, oranges, lemons, and limes are loaded with **vitamin C**, which has an antihistaminic effect that can reduce the nasal symptoms associated with a cold.

Citrus Zing

1 grapefruit
3 oranges
1 lemon
1 lime

1 Juice the fruit: either cut in half and use a citrus juicer, or peel the fruit and feed the segments through a juicer.

2 Serve immediately for the maximum dose of Vitamin C.

Apple and Citrus Zing: If using a juicer, feed 2 crisp apples through the juicer after the citrus fruit.

Cherry and Orange Juice

Large handful of cherries, pitted
3 oranges, peeled and segmented

1 Feed the cherries through a juicer, followed by the orange segments.

2 Pour into a glass and serve.

Cherry and Orange Smoothie: Blend the cherries in a blender until smooth. Squeeze the oranges, add the juice to the blender, and whiz again.

It has been suggested that cherries have **painkilling properties**. One thing is for certain – they are packed with **pectin**, a fibre that can help lower cholesterol, and they are a good source of vitamin C.

love your life

Pineapple Energizer

1 pineapple, peeled, tough core
    removed, and cut into chunks
1 peach, stoned and cut into wedges
115g/4oz/1 cup strawberries, washed
    and hulled
Few blackcurrants
Freshly squeezed orange juice

1 Place the pineapple, strawberries, and
currants in a blender with 125ml/4floz/
½ cup of orange juice; blend until smooth.

2 Add more orange juice to thin to your
desired consistency and serve.

Blue Pineapple Energizer: Use
blueberries in place of the blackcurrants.

Carrots are rich in **beta carotene** and are good for
the immune system, skin, and
eyes. Cardamom is thought to
help fight colds and fever.

Creamy Carrot and Cardamom Dream

6 carrots, trimmed
4 tbsp single (light) cream, low-fat
    fromage frais (yogurt), or quark
Seeds of 4 cardamom pods, crushed

1 Feed the carrots through a juicer.

2 Stir in the cream, fromage frais (yogurt),
or quark; add the cardamom seeds.

3 Pour into a glass to serve.

**Creamy Carrot and Coriander
Dream:** Replace the cardamom with a
small handful of coriander leaves
(cilantro) and feed through the juicer.

Creamy Carrot and Parsley Dream:
Replace the cardamom with a handful of
parsley and feed through the juicer.

Raspberry and Banana Tofu Smoothie

live life to the full

115g/4oz/1cup raspberries
1 small banana, peeled
175g/6oz/¾ cup soft tofu
350ml/12floz/1½ cups freshly squeezed
   orange juice

1 Place the raspberries, banana, and tofu in a blender and blend until smooth.

2 Add the orange juice and blend again.

3 Pour into glasses and serve.

Strawberry and Banana Tofu Smoothie: Replace the raspberries with strawberries.

Blackberry and Banana Tofu Smoothie: Use blackberries instead of raspberries.

Tofu, a good all-round food, is high in protein, calcium, and vitamin E, and low in saturated fats, making it great for strong muscles and bones.

Fruity Beety Beauty

2 beetroots (beets), trimmed
1 large orange, peeled
Small handful fresh raspberries

1 Cut the beetroots (beets) into quarters and feed half through a juicer.

2 Next feed the orange segments through, then the remaining beetroots (beets). Pour the juice into a blender.

3 Add the raspberries to the blender and blend until smooth.

4 Pour into a glass and serve.

Enjoy this juice to boost your immunity. Beetroot is a good source of folate and vitamin C.

Blueberries are full of **antioxidants**, which may slow down the aging process. Yogurt is a good source of calcium.

Blueberry Yog Nog

115g/4oz/1 cup blueberries
225ml/8floz/1cup low-fat natural
  (plain) yogurt
1 tbsp clear honey
1 tbsp sunflower seeds

1 Place the blueberries, yogurt, and honey in a blender and blend until smooth.

2 Pour into glasses and sprinkle with the sunflower seeds.

Raspberry Yog Nog: Use raspberries in place of the blueberries.

Yog Nog with Pumpkin Seeds: Use pumpkin seeds instead of sunflower seeds.

Passion Zoom

1 small mango, peeled, stoned, and
  cut into chunks
1 wedge pineapple, peeled and cut
  into chunks
12fml/4floz/½ cup orange juice
1 passion fruit

1 Place the mango, pineapple, and orange juice in a blender and blend until smooth.

2 Cut the passion fruit in half and scoop out the seeds. Add to the blender and blend briefly.

3 Pour over ice and serve.

Creamy Passion Zoom: Replace the pineapple with a peeled banana.

This refreshing juice is packed full of antioxidants that are perfect for building up your **immune system.**

Grapes and berries
contain sulphur, which is
good for **healthy
skin**.

Grape and Raspberry Glow

225ml/8floz/1cup red grape juice
175g/6oz/1½ cups raspberries

1 Place the fruit in a blender, reserving a few raspberries. Blend until well combined.

2 Push through a nylon sieve to remove seeds if desired.

3 Pour into a glass and top with reserved raspberries.

Green Grapes and Blueberry Glow:
Substitute the ingredients with seedless green grapes and blueberries.

Pineapple has one of the strongest protein-digesting enzymes, bromelain, and melons have diuretic and digestive cleansing properties, making this drink ideal for improving your digestive system and helping to alleviate digestive problems.

Melon, Pineapple, and Mango Smoothie

1 wedge cantaloupe melon, peeled and cut into chunks
1 wedge pineapple, peeled and cut into chunks
½ mango, peeled and cut into chunks
125ml/4floz/½ cup freshly squeezed orange juice
Mango slices to decorate

1 Place all the ingredients in a blender and blend until smooth.

2 Pour over ice, if desired, and decorate with slices of mango.

Fruity Juice: Feed the ingredients through a juicer for a thinner juice drink.

Papaya, Pineapple, and Mango Smoothie: Give the drink even more protein-digesting enzymes by adding a wedge of papaya to the mix.

Minty Tummy Calmer

225g/8oz/2 cups strawberries, hulled
1 lime
2 tbsp freshly chopped mint
1–2 tbsp clear honey or maple syrup
  (optional)

1 Feed the strawberries through a juicer.

2 Squeeze the juice from the lime and stir into the strawberry juice.

3 Stir in the chopped mint. Sweeten with a little honey or maple syrup if desired.

4 Pour into a glass and serve.

Strawberry Tummy Calmer: Add the juice of 1 lemon instead of lime.

Strawberry and Black Pepper Juice

350g/12oz /1½ cups strawberries,
  washed and hulled
2 apples, quartered
¼ tsp crushed black pepper

1 Feed the strawberries and apples through a juicer.

2 Stir in the pepper and serve.

Strawberry and Balsamic Juice: Add ½ tsp balsamic vinegar with the pepper for a fabulous tang.

Strawberries contain the phytochemical ellagic acid, which is believed to help prevent cancer, making this sweet juice a healthy choice.

Fennel and carrot juice creates a popular combination that has been used for centuries as a traditional remedy for poor **eyesight**. This combination is also used to help relieve headaches and may help menopausal or menstrual problems too.

Bright-Eyed Woman

1 fennel bulb, trimmed
3 carrots, trimmed

1 Feed the fennel and carrots through a juicer.

2 Pour into a glass and add ice if required.

Sprouty Bright-Eyed Woman: Add a handful of alfalfa sprouts, which are high in vitamins A, C, and K.

Green Bright-Eyed Woman: Add 1 carrot and ½ an avocado – it is high in vitamin E, which is good for healthy skin.

Berry Booster

Three or four 85g/3oz/¾ cup portions of: strawberries, blackberries, raspberries, blueberries, loganberries, bilberries, or cherries, pitted
A little clear honey (optional)

1 Feed the berries of your choice through a juicer.

2 Sweeten with a little honey if desired.

Berry and Orange Booster: Substitute one portion of berries with 125ml/4floz/½ cup fresh orange juice.

pack a healthy punch

Carrot, Parsnip, and Avocado Blemish Blaster

2 large carrots, trimmed
1 parsnip, trimmed and cut into chunks
1 avocado, peeled and stoned
½ lemon

1 Feed the carrots and parsnips through a juicer.

2 Place the avocado in a blender, then add the carrot, parsnip, and lemon juices. Blend until smooth.

3 Pour into a glass and serve.

Carrot, Apple, and Avocado Smoothie: Use 2 carrots, 1 apple, and the avocado.

This is a good healing juice for people with acne or other skin complaints. The smoothie is high in vitamin E, which is important for healthy skin.

Apple and melons are both great for **detoxing** the body.

Melon, Blackberry, and Apple Detox

¼ wedge galia or honeydew melon, peeled
115g/4oz/1 cup blackberries, washed and hulled
175ml/6 floz/¾ cup apple juice

1 Place the melon and blackberries in a blender with the apple juice and blend until smooth.

2 Pour over ice if desired and serve.

Melon, Raspberry, and Apple Smoothie: Replace the blackberries with raspberries for a lighter smoothie.

say bye-bye to muscle aches

Rosemary Red

200g/7oz/1½ cups raspberries
115g/4oz/1 cup redcurrants
115g/4oz/1 cup blackcurrants
125ml/4floz/½ cup orange or grape juice
1 tsp freshly chopped rosemary

1 Place all the ingredients in a blender
and blend until smooth. If desired push
through a nylon sieve to remove seeds.

2 Pour into glasses and serve.

Ginger Red: Add 2.5cm/1 inch piece
of peeled and grated ginger root in
place of the rosemary.

Tarragon Red: Use tarragon in place
of rosemary.

Berries are good sources of
proanthocyanins and
vitamin C, which are required for a
healthy immune system. They may
also have properties that protect
against cancer.

Cold Buster

2 kiwi fruits, peeled and cut into wedges
2 apples, cut into wedges
2 tbsp lemon juice
1 tsp echinacea (optional)

1 Feed the fruit through a juicer.

2 Stir in the lemon juice and echinacea;
serve immediately.

Pear Cold Buster: Replace the apples
with pears.

Echinacea (available from
health food shops) helps relieve
the symptoms of colds and
flu. The antiseptic properties
found in lemon juice are also good
for fighting off colds.

Apricot Hormone Juice

225ml/8floz/1 cup soy milk
3 tbsp probiotic yogurt
1tsp tahini
6 apricots, stoned
Few toasted sesame seeds

1 Place the milk, yogurt, tahini, and apricots in a blender and blend until smooth.

2 Pour into glasses, sprinkle the sesame seeds on top, and serve.

Peach Hormone Juice: Use 1 peach in place of the apricots.

This juice is high in calcium and the apricots provide potassium. This drink has a balancing effect that may help when hormones are affecting your mood.

The sour flavor of the gooseberries is counteracted by the sweetness of the kiwi fruits in this immune-boosting juice, which is a good source of vitamin C, potassium, and bioflavonoids.

Gooseberry and Kiwi Juice

6 kiwi fruits, cut into wedges
150g/5oz/1 cup gooseberries
1 sweet apple, quartered

1 Feed the ingredients through a juicer.

2 Pour into a glass and serve.

Gooseberry, Pear, and Kiwi Juice: Omit the apple and use 4 kiwi fruits and 2 quartered pears.

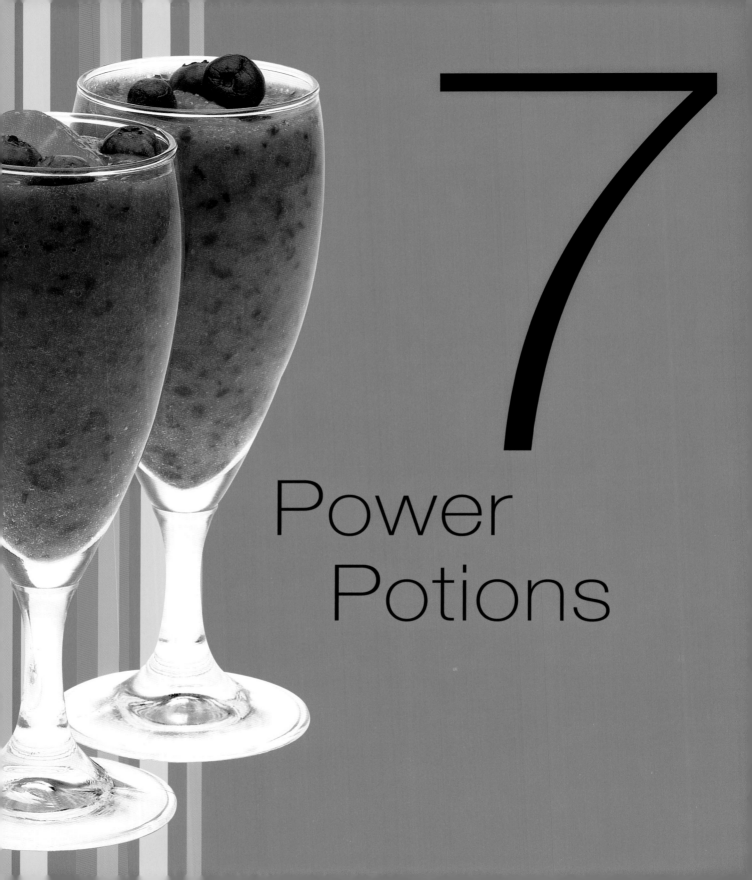

7

Power Potions

Sweet Potato and Cabbage Energizer

2 carrots, trimmed
1 small sweet potato, peeled and cut
    into chunks
½ small savoy cabbage, shredded
Handful of seaweed
2 tsp sesame seeds

1 Place the carrots, sweet potato, cabbage, and seaweed in a blender and blend until smooth.

2 Pour into glasses, sprinkle the sesame seeds on top, and serve.

Oriental Energizer: Replace the cabbage with ½ medium head of Chinese cabbage and add a handful of pak choy.

Seaweed is a rich source of minerals and the sesame seeds are an excellent source of energy, making this combination a good drink for anyone who is experiencing stress and fatigue.

This energizing drink is the perfect boost when coping with a work overload. It's packed with vitamins A, C, and E and potassium and will help you to improve your mental capacity to concentrate.

Rocket Booster

2 carrots, trimmed
1 kiwi fruit
1 large tomato
Handful of rocket (arugula)
Handful of watercress
2 apples, quartered

1 Cut two slices from a tomato and reserve. Feed the remaining ingredients through a juicer.

2 Pour into glasses, decorate with the tomato slices, and serve.

Spinach Booster: Replace the rocket (arugula) with a handful of spinach.

Juicy Joints

½ mango, peeled and stoned
1 banana, peeled
1 apple, quartered
1 pear, quartered
225g/8oz/2 cups strawberries, washed
　　and hulled
2 tsp tahini

1 Reserve a strawberry and a couple of slices of banana. Feed the remaining fruit through a juicer.

2 Dilute the tahini with a little hot water if required and stir into the juice.

3 Pour into glasses and decorate with reserved fruit.

Juicy Blueberry: Replace the strawberries with blueberries.

This vitamin-packed drink will help keep your muscles going through the day. Mangoes are a rich source of beta carotene, potassium, and iron. They are also high in pectin, a fibre that can help to control blood cholesterol.

Packed with **protein** and calcium, this is a great shake for those who want to build body weight rather than reduce it. Muscles weigh more than fat.

Muscle Magic

1 banana, peeled
½ papaya, peeled and seeded
115g/4oz/½ cup silken tofu
225ml/8floz/1 cup whole-milk natural
   (plain) yogurt
1 tsp wheat germ
Slices papaya to serve

1 Place all the ingredients, except the slices of papaya, in a blender and blend to combine.

2 Pour into glasses, decorate with the papaya slices, and serve immediately.

Dairy-Free Muscle Magic: Use a soy yogurt instead of a dairy yogurt.

A perfect drink for before or after **exercise**, wheat germ has the B vitamins, vitamin E, proteins, and minerals. Linseeds have essential fatty acids (good oils), and banana and avocado are good for supplying energy.

Easy Exerciser

2 tbsp wheat germ
1 small banana, peeled
½ avocado, peeled and stoned
125g/4oz/½ cup natural (plain) yogurt
1 tbsp linseeds
2 tbsp lime juice
6 tbsp orange juice

1 Place all the ingredients in a blender and blend until well combined.

2 Pour into a glass and sprinkle with a few more linseeds if desired.

Banana Exerciser: Replace the avocado with ½ of a peeled banana.

Hearty Red Pepper and Sweet Potato

2 red peppers, seeded and cut
  into strips
1 clove garlic
Few basil leaves
1 medium sweet potato, peeled and
  cut into chunks
2 carrots

1 Feed the vegetables in the order listed through a juicer.

2 Pour over ice and serve.

Hearty Yellow Pepper and Sweet Potato: Use yellow peppers instead of the red peppers.

Hearty Green Pepper and Sweet Potato: For a slightly sharper juice, use green peppers instead of red peppers.

Sweet potatoes are a rich source of **beta carotene**, which can be converted to vitamin A in the body. They are also packed with vitamin C and potassium. Garlic is good for the **heart**.

Broccoli has almost as much **calcium** as milk, so this juice is ideal for boosting calcium levels in people on a dairy-free diet. Calcium is an essential aid for women in helping to prevent osteoporosis.

Calcium Booster

175g/6oz/1 cup broccoli florets
2 crisp apples, quartered
1 tbsp lime or lemon juice

1 Feed the broccoli and apples through a juicer and stir in the lime juice.

2 Pour into a glass and serve.

Creamy Calcium Booster: Boost the calcium content further by adding 2 tbsp natural (plain) yogurt.

Love your Heart

½ cucumber, peeled
1 avocado, peeled and stoned
Celery stick to stir

1 Feed the cucumber through a juicer.

2 Place the juice and the avocado in a blender and blend until smooth.

3 Pour into a glass, add the celery stick, and serve immediately.

Cucumber can help **lower blood pressure.**

As well as being important for cardiovascular health, the avocado may also help to keep you looking good – it is packed with vitamin E, which is good for the skin.

Purple Power

½ small red cabbage, thickly shredded
2 pears, quartered
1 tbsp lemon juice

1 Feed the cabbage and pears through
a juicer. Stir in the lemon juice.

2 Pour into glasses and serve.

Fennel Power: Feed ½ a trimmed
fennel bulb through the juicer after
the pears.

Pears are a great energizer,
and they are combined here with
red cabbage for a great tasting
power juice. Cabbage is loaded with
vitamin C, especially red cabbage,
and may help prevent colon cancer.

With plenty of the B vitamins,
this juice is sure to boost your
brain power.

Memory Master

2 fresh dates, stoned and chopped
4 dried apricots, stoned and chopped
2 tbsp seedless raisins
225ml/8floz/1 cup natural (plain) yogurt
1–2 tsp brewer's yeast

1 Place the dates, apricots, and raisins
in a blender with 6 tbsp water and
purée until smooth.

2 Add the yogurt and brewer's yeast and
blend again.

3 Pour into a glass and serve.

Wheat Master: Replace the brewer's
yeast with wheat germ.

Red Berry and Willing

115g/4oz/1 cup strawberries, washed
  and hulled
115g/4oz/1 cup blueberries
1 tsp ginseng powder (optional)
2.5cm/1 inch piece of ginger root,
  peeled
1 tbsp clear honey
125ml/4floz/½ cup freshly squeezed
  orange juice

1 Reserve a strawberry and a few
   blueberries. Place all the ingredients in
   a blender and blend until smooth.

2 Pour into glasses, decorate with the
   reserved fruit, and serve.

Currants, Berry, and Willing: Add
some redcurrants and blackcurrants for
a super fruity smoothie.

Blueberries are a good source of zinc
and other nutrients that can give a
boost to the **reproductive
hormones** of both men and
women. Strawberries have long been
thought of as the fruit of love.

Broccoli, carrots, and cucumber are good sources of zinc, which is vital for healthy sperm.

One for the Men

4 carrots, trimmed
85g/3oz/⅓ cup broccoli florets
¼ cucumber, peeled
4 tbsp ground almonds
1 tsp pumpkin seeds
1 tsp sunflower seeds

1 Feed the carrots, broccoli, and cucumber through a juicer.

2 Stir in the ground almonds.

3 Pour into glasses, sprinkle the seeds on top, and serve.

Another for the Men: Replace the broccoli with a handful of watercress.

Pineapple is a good source of thiamine, riboflavin, and manganese, and these are all important for energy production.

On the Go

½ pineapple, peeled and cut into chunks
1 large banana, peeled
115g/4oz/1 cup strawberries, washed
   and hulled

1 Place all the ingredients in a blender and blend until smooth.

2 Pour into glasses and serve.

Stay On the Go: Add to the blender a little cooked brown rice for slow-released energy. Thin with a little water or apple juice if desired.

Sunny Tofu Smoothie

225g/8oz/1 cup soft tofu
225g/8oz/2 cups mixed berries such as
   blackberries, raspberries, strawberries,
   and red or blackcurrants
1 tbsp lime juice
Pineapple juice
1 tbsp sunflower seeds

1 Place the tofu, berries, lime juice, and a splash of pineapple juice in a blender and blend until smooth.

2 Add extra pineapple juice until you have a smoothie of your preferred thickness.

3 Pour into glasses and sprinkle with sunflower seeds to serve.

Orange Tofu Smoothie: Use orange juice in place of the pineapple juice.

Tofu, made from soy beans, is a great vegetarian source of protein and iron, and it has the B vitamins, calcium, potassium, and other minerals, making it an energizing drink.